The Golden Rules
Solution Diary

Compiled by:

E. J. Ezekiel

The Golden Rules Solution Diary
Copyright: © 2010 E. J. Ezekiel

+353 87 282 0197, +353 87 953 3613

Emails:
Ezekiel@faithrestoration.info
hisjustice@ymail.com
www.faithrestoration.info

ISBN: 978-0-9564927-3-9
Published by: Lacepoint Publishing
Book Design & Cover illustration by Lacepoint Designs Ireland

Printed in Ireland

Acknowledgements

I give God all the glory and the honour for giving birth to this book, "Solution Diary". I thank Him for His Spirit of revelation, inspiration, wisdom and understanding that indwelled me throughout the time of compiling this diary.

I also want to say a big thank you to Cian Fogarty and Daniel Noe for their immense support for the work done on this "Solution Diary".

Dedication

This "Solution Diary" is dedicated to every child of God that strongly desires the truth of the word of God and wants to grow spiritually by it. The inspirational sayings in this book are a good tool for you and it will bless your life.

Contents

Chapter	Page

Introduction

Solution diary is a compilation of inspirational sayings from the word of God. It is powerful, and can transform and change the life of anyone who reads them, takes them to heart and decides to do something about them. It is quotations from the word of God, easy to understand and clear in presentation. It is powerful enough to warm your heart, stir your heart, and kick your heart, ready to manifest Christlike character in your life.

It is relevant for everyday Christian living and is good for desired Christian growth. For the weak and lukewarm Christian, it will strengthen you, motivate you, and cause you to step out of your comfort zone and reach out for something greater. For the person who is hungry for the practicality of the word of God, and wants to pass it to others, it is a good tool to be used!

The inspired sayings in the book is a depth of knowledge in the word of God, it is more like the words of a preacher and is powerful enough to change lives. It is a challenge to the life that is not very productive towards a life of righteousness and power.

Solution diary is also a volume of gracious, righteous rules in the word of God, that is golden and worthy of following. It is the word of God oriented and originated.

1

Discipline and Reward

Discipline, a very tough investment, that yields a very good profit; it is a gold that goes through the refiner's fire, but comes out to be a pure gold. It is a clay in the hands of the potter that turns out to be what the potter intended it to be originally, after the process.

Discipline is like a house where it is not comfortable for you to stay now, "but will be the best place for you to stay afterwards!" If you buy discipline, you have made a very good decision and you will have a good profit, "but if you ignore discipline, you will have diminishing returns." Turn over the page now and let's begin!

If you become a poor person, don't blame anybody! It may be because you are not disciplined! Prov. 10:4

◆•••◆

It will be difficult for you to live an effective prayer life, until you discipline yourself! Dan. 6:10

◆•••◆

Before you discipline others, discipline yourself first and you will have a good result. Matt. 7:5

◆•••◆

Until you accept God's discipline, "you can never be counted as one of His children." Heb. 12:5-8

◆•••◆

Until you discipline your child, shame will always locate your house! Prov. 29:15

◆•••••••••••••••••••••••••••••••••••••••◆

If you are not disciplined, it will be difficult for you to control your sex drive! 2 Sam. 11:2-4

◆•••••••••••••••••••••••••••••••••••••••◆

Your love for your children is questionable if you refuse to discipline them! But if you love your children, you will not hesitate to discipline them! Prov. 13:24

◆•••••••••••••••••••••••••••••••••••••••◆

There is nothing wrong with physical punishment when necessary; it is a way of discipline. Prov. 20:30

◆•••••••••••••••••••••••••••••••••••••••◆

Don't sleep when you are supposed to be working, and you will have food to eat tomorrow! Prov. 24:30-34

◆••••••••••••••••••••••••••••••••••••••◆

Cursing and swearing is not a form of discipline, you will be wearied out very soon, "but believing and confessing the word of God, is a discipline that pays." <u>*Righteous Rule*</u>

◆••••••••••••••••••••••••••••••••••••••◆

There is some foolishness in the heart of a child that will never go, until you apply discipline! Prov. 22:15

◆••••••••••••••••••••••••••••••••••••••◆

Count yourself among the privileged people that God disciplined; because you need it for your success! Ps. 119:75

◆••••••••••••••••••••••••••••••••••••••◆

Without discipline it will be difficult for you to self-control your life! Prov. 25:28

◆•••◆

Until you discipline yourself; you may not be able to endure to the end! Matt. 24:13

◆•••◆

You have counted yourself among the fools, if you refuse your parents discipline! Prov. 15:5

◆•••◆

It takes discipline for you to finish your Christian journey well! Without it, you may be disqualified at the end! 1 Cor. 9:27

◆•••◆

If you refuse God's discipline; you have rejected his love which is far better than discipline! Rev. 3:19

NOTES

2

Sowing and Reaping

God has designed this earth to be a place of sowing and reaping. God in His infinite wisdom knows the end from the beginning. He knows what comes out of everything that is done here on earth. God always knows what will be the outcome of anything before He asks us to do it, even when we don't understand it.

When we talk about "sowing and reaping", it is difficult for us to understand it in an alphabetical setting of it. In the sense that, it is the letter (R) which is the beginning letter for "reap" that comes first before the letter (S) which is the beginning letter for "sow". Everything about God is all about faith, because "without faith it is impossible to please God." (Heb. 11:6)

God has given us "Human beings" some measures of faith, when dealing with this subject, sowing and reaping. We have to understand that it is for everybody, the believers and unbelievers. To the believers, it is a principle in life and a powerful revelation from God. To the unbelievers, it is only a principle in life that is in operation, which if applied will have a result after it.

God has given everybody a measure of faith that is why I believe anybody can do something about this subject, sowing and reaping. It is not natural to see "reaping comes before sowing", that is why it takes faith of any amount to see it that way. The simple reason why it is so is "faith." It is a picture of a farmer who sees the harvest before sowing the seed. It is a "faith thing."

Whatever seed that is sown, will determine the outcome of what will be harvested. The subject of sowing and reaping also conveys the idea of negative and positive, evil or good. This is in the sense of whatever you sow, the same shall you reap.

As long as we are in this place called "the earth", sowing and reaping, cold and heat, summer and winter will never stop. Gen. 8:22

◆ ⋯⋯⋯⋯⋯⋯⋯⋯⋯⋯⋯⋯⋯⋯⋯⋯ ◆

God is a just God; He knows how to give to anyone what they deserve, be it evil or good! Jer. 17:10

◆ ⋯⋯⋯⋯⋯⋯⋯⋯⋯⋯⋯⋯⋯⋯⋯⋯ ◆

Godly people find life; but untimely death is always knocking at the door of the evil people. Prov. 11:19

◆ ⋯⋯⋯⋯⋯⋯⋯⋯⋯⋯⋯⋯⋯⋯⋯⋯ ◆

If you give what you have, more will be given to you! But if you hold back what you have, you may be creating a hole in your pocket that will cause you to lose everything! Prov. 11:24

◆ ⋯⋯⋯⋯⋯⋯⋯⋯⋯⋯⋯⋯⋯⋯⋯⋯ ◆

Don't worry about your tears and pain when planting your seed; because you are going to have a harvest of joy thereafter. Ps. 126:5, 6

◆ • ◆

If you are in the business of helping others in their time of need; God will also be in the business of helping you in your time of need. Prov. 11:25

◆ • ◆

If you refuse to use whatever God has given you to better the life of other people; God will not only take it back from you, but you will be counted among the useless people ever to walk the face of this earth! Matt. 25:24-30

◆ • ◆

If you are a giver, you have entered into God's business of multiplication! Luke 6:38

◆••◆

As a peacemaker, you are sowing a seed of peace and you are going to reap "not just a harvest of peace, but of all goodness." Jas. 3:18

◆••◆

Whatever you give for the work of God to be done, will determine what God will give you, to get your work done! 2 Cor. 9:6

◆••◆

If your business is to go about planting the seed of troubles; it will not be too long before you reap a harvest of troubles and pain. Job 4:8

◆••◆

Whatever you want people to do for you, do the same for them! This is the word of God fulfilled. Matt. 7:12

◆ • ◆

If you give to the poor, your blessings are guaranteed; but if you see the poor and turn away, you could be in the worst situation than the poor tomorrow! Prov. 28:27

◆ • ◆

If you are a seeker of good things favour will locate you; but if you seek for evil you have invited troubles and disaster! Prov. 11:27

◆ • ◆

There is no amount of gifts given to the man of God that is too much! Considering what he has given also, which is the word of God. 1 Cor. 9:11

◆••◆

If you are a wise person, when it comes to the work of God, give generously; for whatever is put into the hand of God will definitely multiply. 2 Cor. 9:7-9

◆••◆

There is a wonderful blessing that await those who sow the seed of the word of God to the life of others, and those who help to harvest that seed. John 4:36

◆••◆

If you are open to the word of God, divine understanding and knowledge will be your portion; but if you ignore it, you have voted for great loss. Matt 13:12

◆••◆

Don't mistreat the poor people by not paying them when they work for you, because they will cry out to God and He will hold their cry against you! Jas. 5:4

◆ . . . . ◆

If you want friends; simply sow the seed of friendship, and you will have many friends. <u>Righteous Rule</u>

◆ . . . . ◆

Sow the seed of time: if you want more time given to you concerning anything! <u>Righteous Rule</u>

◆ . . . . ◆

You get out of life what you put into it. <u>Righteous Rule</u>

◆ . . . . ◆

God is not a joker! "He is very serious concerning sowing and reaping" whatever you sow, the same shall you reap! Gal. 6:7

NOTES

3

Pride vs. Humbleness

Pride! A state of being high minded or being boastful, a state of seeing oneself above others. It is accrediting personal glory to oneself or crowning oneself instead of others. Pride! If it is not being mindful of, can result in being proud, which is always used in Scripture in the bad sense of arrogance, disdainful, which is also being proud and is always in a negative sense.

This is an attitude contrary to the character of God from the very beginning, which He hates. Pride in a negative sense always has bad consequences after it. But "humbleness" which is the very opposite of pride, is a state of lowliness of mind or humility of mind which is an attitude, that represents the very character of God.

Humbleness, in a true sense, most of the time appears to be a weak type of attitude, but in real sense is powerful. Humbleness, as a character always discomfits pride at the end. Whenever "pride vs. humbleness" is in competition, humbleness always wins!

*Humble yourself "before God does",
because you will never like the
experience! Dan. 4:33*

◆•••◆

*If you don't stop your pride now; it will
drive you down the path to wickedness,
which will bring judgement upon your
life! Ezek. 7:10, 11*

◆•••◆

*A proud person may be capable of
oppressing the poor! But he is doing this
to his own detriment. Ps. 10:2*

◆•••◆

*If you are a person that fears the Lord;
there is no doubt you will hate whatever
is done in pride and arrogance. Prov.
8:13*

◆•••◆

Your pride will only cause you to be disgraced at the end; but with humility, your wisdom is unlimited! Prov. 11:2

◆••◆

Until you humble yourself; God will continue to distance Himself from you! Ps. 138:6

◆••◆

You will be opened to more troubles and calamity; if you refuse to submit and humble yourself before God! Exod. 10:3

◆••◆

You can never be tempted with what you are contented with! <u>Righteous Rule</u>

◆••◆

Swallow your pride, it contains no calories! <u>Righteous Rule</u>

◆••◆

If you humble yourself before God, you will receive His mercy and forgiveness; but if you don't, you will die in your sin. 2 Chron. 7:14

◆•••••••••••••••••••••••••••••••••••◆

Very soon! Pride will take you on a long journey where you will lose all that you have, before coming back home; if you don't humble yourself now! Obad. 1:3, 4

◆•••••••••••••••••••••••••••••••••••◆

God will surely humble the proud! Don't let it be you! Isaiah 5:15

◆•••••••••••••••••••••••••••••••••••◆

It is pride that will make you enter into unnecessary argument with people, because you want to prove yourself; but if you are wise you will be able to listen to other people's opinion. Prov. 13:10

◆•••••••••••••••••••••••••••••••••••◆

Pride will only lead you to a sudden fall very soon, if you don't humble yourself! Prov. 16:18

◆•••◆

One of the easiest accesses that the "devil" has to a person's life is through pride! 1 Tim. 3:6

◆•••◆

It will be very difficult for you to do the will of God; if you have pride in you. 1 John 2:16, 17

◆•••◆

God is powerful and he is the most High and High and High… but He is very low and near to those who are humble in heart! Isaiah 57:15

◆•••◆

The final destination of a person who walks in pride is humiliation; but with humility, you will always find yourself among the great! Prov. 29:23

◆• •◆

If you want to know what true humbleness is like; look at the life of the little children, and you will understand! Matt. 18:4

◆• •◆

Those who want a true promotion in life, know what the answer is! It is humbleness! Matt. 23:12

◆• •◆

The greatest form of humbleness is dying to oneself; this kind of humbleness has the greatest reward after it. Phil. 2:8, 9

◆• •◆

Humbleness will make you take your eyes off yourself, and look unto God; because He knows how to take care of you. Jas. 4:10

◆......................................◆

God has made Himself an enemy to the proud! But to those who are humble, His favour is guaranteed! 1 Pet. 5:5

◆......................................◆

With humbleness you will serve God effectively; but with pride, you will have a lot of frustrations! Acts 20:19, 20

◆......................................◆

"Pride and Selfishness" are two bad friends; but humbleness is a friend of everybody. Phil. 2:3

◆......................................◆

Humbleness! Is one of the true essences of a believer's walk with the Lord and other believers! Col. 3:12

◆ • ◆

God knows how to lift you up! When you humble yourself! 1 Pet. 5:6

◆ • ◆

Disgrace is not far away from the person who walks in pride; but the person who is humble will be honoured. Luke 14:11

◆ • ◆

If you want to find a true rest and quietness for your soul; then imitate the life of Christ; "It is a life of humbleness and gentleness." Matt. 11:29

◆ • ◆

With pride, it will be difficult for you to have an audience with God; but with humbleness, you are qualified for His favour. Jas. 4:6

◆•••◆

Where there is pride! People will find it difficult to agree with each other; but with humility, understanding and love will thrive! 1 Pet. 3:8

◆•••◆

You are among the list of people that God has decided to bring down if you walk in pride and arrogance; but with lowliness of mind, God will lift you up. Luke 1:51, 52

◆•••◆

It is pride that will make you think you know more than everybody! But with "humility" you will be open for more knowledge, wisdom and understanding! Rom. 12:16

◆••◆

If you humble yourself, you will be lifted up; but if you first lift yourself up, you will be brought down; it is as simple as that! Matt. 23:12

NOTES

4

Integrity Precedes Honour

Integrity; it is to live a life of honesty or to be honest. It is to be whole or to show wholeness in all dealings and ramifications. It is to live in complete honesty, which as a result, honour is obtained. "Honest", from the Greek word called "kalos" which is to be good, admirable or becoming admirable. It has also the ethical meaning of what is fair, right, and honourable, of a conduct that deserves to be esteemed.

To be honest in all your dealings, is to live a life of integrity. Honest is also from a Latin word "honestus", from the word "honos", which is to honour. This has the same meaning as "honest." Honour comes as a result of the life of "integrity", first taking its place.

Integrity is a lifestyle that will bring happiness to you; because it is one of the characters of God. Ps. 119:1

◆•••◆

Integrity and honesty, carries with it "protection all the way" because it is a character that can sustains those who possess it! Ps. 25:21

◆•••◆

It is the power of integrity that will keep you standing in the face of trials; even when you don't know why! But you know there is a God who knows! Job 2:9, 10

◆•••◆

Integrity and honesty! That is what it takes to be a true worshipper and a true follower of the Lord. Ps. 15:1-5

◆•••◆

If you are honest, and a person who walks in integrity; then you will not only experience the presence of God in your life, but will have all the good things contained in His presence. Isaiah 33:15, 16

◆ • ◆

You will not lack any good thing in this life; if you are honest and a person who walks in integrity. Ps. 84:11

◆ • ◆

Walk in honesty, and you will have a very smooth journey; walk in dishonesty, and you will have a continuous accident that will eventually wreck your life! Ps. 11:3

◆ • ◆

Your case will always be with a difference with God; if you walk in integrity! Ps. 7:8

◆•••◆

It is very ease to give in to compromise in the face of trials; if you are not a person of integrity. Ps. 26:1

◆•••◆

A life of honesty will put you on a top list and cause people to respect you! Acts 6:3

◆•••◆

When you think about good things that are true, honourable and good! It will surely reflect in your life! Phil. 4:8

◆•••◆

Integrity will make you take your stand for what you know is the right thing;

even when you are faced with dangers or death. Job 27:5, 6

◆•••◆

Integrity! Is a form of protection for those who put their trust in God! Ps. 25:21

◆•••◆

Not returning "evil for evil, but good for evil" is not a sign of weakness; it is a sign of honourable character that you possess! Rom. 12:17

◆•••◆

The way you handle the things of God, will determine how honourable you are before God and His people. 2 Cor. 8:21

◆•••◆

Your integrity will make you maintain your stand in obeying the word of God;

*even when people persecute you. Ps.
119:86, 87*

◆••••••••••••••••••••••••••••••••••••••◆

*Determination is a quality of character
that will take you to a very good end;
because you are a person of integrity. Ps.
119:112*

◆••••••••••••••••••••••••••••••••••••••◆

*Stability will drive you to honesty;
honesty will drive you to success,
success is a mark of fruitfulness! Luke
8:15*

◆••••••••••••••••••••••••••••••••••••••◆

*If you are honest and a person of
integrity in your dealings; people will
always vote for you! Rom. 13:13*

◆••••••••••••••••••••••••••••••••••••••◆

If you are a leader with integrity, there is no doubt you will want your followers to be the people of integrity also! 2 Cor. 13:7

◆• •◆

There is no doubt that people who suffered for the work of Christ to be done will be honoured by others! Phil. 2:29, 30

◆• •◆

There is a guaranteed protection to those who walk on the path of integrity! Prov. 2:7

◆• •◆

Let your yes be yes, and your no be no, and people will always trust you! Jas. 5:12

◆• •◆

If your heart's desire is to live an honest and honourable life; God will help you to achieve that desire! Heb. 13:18

NOTES

5

Wisdom is Powerful

Wisdom! One of the attributes of God that is so powerful in operation, one of the ways God does things or wants things to be done. It is first attributed to God, before it is attributed to man, because God is the author of wisdom. Wisdom, from the Greek word "sophia", is an insight into the true nature of things. It is also "phronesis" from the root word "sophia". While "sophia" is theoretical, "phronesis" is practical. It is the ability to discern modes of action with a view to their results.

Wisdom is an indelible character that is credible to those who possess it. It is a mark of quality of life that has the ability to break any barrier and cross any border of difficulties. Where there is wisdom, it will be difficult for people to fall into all kinds of confusion and uncertainty. Wisdom is the ability to get understanding concerning things, it is also the ability to make good judgment. Wisdom is a back-up power behind every good decision and discretion. Life is easy and enjoyable where wisdom is in operation!

True wisdom is obtained only through the fear of God; and to have real understanding is to forsake all forms of evil! Job 28:28

◆••◆

When you revere and obey God, you have laid a good foundation in your life, "which is a true wisdom" and as a result, you will be rewarded! Ps. 111:10

◆••◆

You are like someone who has found a good wife, if you embrace wisdom and your protection is guaranteed through her! Prov. 4:6

◆••◆

If you live your life with wisdom; you will be well guided on your pilgrimage here on earth! Prov. 4:12

◆••◆

Wisdom obtained through the fear of God, will teach you what to do; when you are faced with an immoral woman who wants to have sex with you by force! Gen. 39:9-12

◆••••••••••••••••••••••••••••••••••••••◆

It is wisdom that will help you to avoid the shame of building a house without completion! Prov. 24:27

◆••••••••••••••••••••••••••••••••••••••◆

Wisdom! Will not only bring you good things of life; but it has the power to save your life if you have it! Eccl. 7:12

◆••••••••••••••••••••••••••••••••••••••◆

It is better to have wisdom than riches! Because riches may disappear, but wisdom will help you to find it again! Prov. 23:45

◆••••••••••••••••••••••••••••••••••••••◆

Wisdom is not rooted in doing what pleases people; but is rooted in doing "the will of God." Matt. 11:19

◆••••••••••••••••••••••••••••••••••••••◆

If you find Christ Jesus, you have found wisdom; He is the wisdom of God, made manifest! 1 Cor. 1:30

◆••••••••••••••••••••••••••••••••••••••◆

It is only your wisdom in God that will distinguish you from other people; and will cause you to do extraordinary things! Matt. 13:54

◆••••••••••••••••••••••••••••••••••••••◆

If you want to be rich in every area of your life, "then find wisdom", because riches and wisdom move together, and God is a supplier of both of them! Rom. 11:33

◆••••••••••••••••••••••••••••••••••••••◆

Don't say you have wisdom, when you are not walking in love and living in peace with others; true wisdom is full of love, peace and mercy for others. Jas. 3:17

◆ • ◆

Pay any price to get wisdom; because wisdom in itself is more expensive, and will pay you back more than you have paid! Prov. 3:14

◆ • ◆

Wisdom has the power to lengthen your life, if you welcome it in your life; but if you refuse it, you have voted for a short life! Prov. 9:11, 12

◆ • ◆

When you operate in the wisdom of God; it will make you a man of God, and a man of the people! Luke 2:52

All the fullness of wisdom is in Christ Jesus; because God has made it so for our benefit! 1 Cor. 1:30

With the wisdom of God in your life; you can never run out of the right words against your enemies who accuse you wrongly! Luke 21:15

When God blesses you with wisdom; favour with people will be unlimited! Acts 7:10

It is better to search for wisdom, than searching for gold; because wisdom is more valuable than gold, and understanding is more precious than silver! Prov. 16:16

◆•••◆

God's type of wisdom often looks foolish in the eyes of the world; but to His people, is a powerful tool to be used in bringing salvation to others! 1 Cor. 1:21

◆•••◆

It is only the wisdom of God in operation, which has the power to bring two opposite people together; that can never do that on their own! Eph. 3:10

◆•••◆

Wisdom is so important concerning the things of God; for it will help you to understand and know the things of God better! Col. 1:9

◆•••◆

There are some things you can never do without wisdom! One of which is, understanding and solving the mystery in the word of God! Rev. 13:18

◆•••••••••••••••••••••••••••••••••••••••◆

If you lack wisdom! Seek for it and you will find it! Jas. 1:5

NOTES

6

Wickedness equals to no Peace

Wickedness! A state of being filled with an unimaginable bad feeling, bad thought, bad idea, bad emotion, bad deeds and bad actions against another. Wickedness! A state of evil conception in the heart which leads to evil action against another person. Wickedness, from the Greek word called "kakia" which sounds so ugly and which also I believe sounds so ugly in other languages of the world. "Kakia", which in its context is rendered evil or wickedness. It is a state of being sinful, evil, mischievous and spiteful. It is a state of restlessness and lack of peace because of the wickedness!

God is righteous and just, that He will never destroy the godly together with the wicked! Gen. 18:25

◆••◆

If you turn away from your wickedness and turn to God, He will definitely pardon you, "but if you do not, you will have what you bargained for." Isaiah 55:7

◆••◆

If you are for God, continue to follow Him, because if you stop and turn your back on Him, "it is a form of wickedness" and it only brings punishment! Jer. 2:19

◆••◆

God is always in rescue operation to the godly, but the wicked is not in his list! Prov. 11:8

◆••◆

The heart of the wicked person is filled with deceit and confusion; but the heart of the godly is a container of joy and peace. Prov. 12:20

◆••◆

With godliness, you will have a smooth sail in this life; but wickedness will cause you to "always" have storm and rough sail in life! Prov. 13:6

◆••◆

Those who love God will enjoy His protections; but the wicked is destined for destruction. Ps. 145:20

◆••◆

Decide not to take part in any form of wickedness and you will be a candidate to the blessings of God. Jer. 14:20

◆•••◆

If you are in position to warn the wicked person but refuse to do that, you will be the one to pay for their wickedness! Ezek. 3:18

◆•••◆

You have no right to speak the word of God; if you still harbour wickedness in your heart! Ps. 50:16

◆•••◆

The wicked man is always guilty and that is why he is always on the run even when no one is pursuing him; but the godly is always bold to face anything. Prov. 28:1

◆•••◆

If you see how disastrous the wicked people end their journey; you will never worry yourself when they get rich and live in luxury! Ps. 49:16, 17

◆••••••••••••••••••••••••••••••••••••••◆

The soul of the righteous is always satisfied; but the soul of the wicked will continue to hunger! Prov. 13:25

◆••••••••••••••••••••••••••••••••••••••◆

God has determined the end of the wicked, "it is the fire of punishment and the hot wind of terror that will blow on them." Ps. 11:6

◆••••••••••••••••••••••••••••••••••••••◆

The wicked man will surely be caught up with what he dreads upon, but the hope of the godly will not be caught off! Prov. 10:24

◆••••••••••••••••••••••••••••••••••••••◆

Those who fear God will have a long and satisfied life; but the life of the wicked will be cut short in misery! Prov. 10:30

◆••◆

All that the wicked hope for in this life will be gone and perish when they die; because they only put their trust in the things of this life, and not in God! Prov. 11:7

◆••◆

It will not be too long before the wicked come to terms with his fate, which is "eternal suffering", when he is finally separated from the godly. Matt 13:49, 50

◆••◆

The true nature of the wicked person is unforgiveness toward other peoples, even when he himself is forgiven by others. Matt. 18:32, 33

◆ ∙∙ ◆

The godly has assurance of looking forward to a happy life, but the wicked will always expect wrath and punishment! Prov. 11:23

◆ ∙∙ ◆

Even though a wicked person knows what is good, he has a vow not to do it, and that is why he is bound for destruction! Prov. 21:7

◆ ∙∙ ◆

A wicked man has many names, one of which is "selfishness", because he will never do something that will be of benefit to others! Matt. 25:26

◆ ∙∙ ◆

There is a sure tragedy that awaits anyone who refuses to turn from his wickedness! Acts 8:22

◆•••••••••••••••••••••••••••••••••••••••◆

There is always help for the godly; buy the wicked will continue to receive judgment from God! 2 Pet. 2:9

◆•••••••••••••••••••••••••••••••••••••••◆

Even though the wicked can be seen now carrying out their wicked act, "don't worry", because very soon they will be gone and never to be found again! Ps. 37:10

◆•••••••••••••••••••••••••••••••••••••••◆

God will never abandon the children of the godly; but the children of the wicked cannot stand His sight, they will be destroyed by it! Ps. 37:28

◆•••••••••••••••••••••••••••••••••••••••◆

There is no peace for the wicked, "says the Lord", not me! Isaiah 57:21

NOTES

7

Holiness equals to God

Hagiasmos, the Greek word translated "holiness", is also rendered sanctification, which is a separation unto God. The result of this kind of separation is for a special benefit to those who separated themselves. "Sanctification", is also a state predetermined by God for believers, into which in grace, He calls them and in which they begin their Christian course and so pursue it. (Definition derived from Vine's Expository Dictionary.)

Holiness is also attributed to Christ, in the days of His flesh as living in the body. But He is distinguished from all mere human beings. Christ also possesses the Spirit of holiness and His resurrection from the dead marked Him out as the Son of God. Believers are to be "perfecting holiness in the fear of God", bringing holiness to the predestined end as Christ did and as a result they may be found "unblameable in holiness through Christ."

Holiness in itself is the very character of God in existence, and should be the character and the lifestyle of those who want to be part of God. Perfecting holiness as believers is the "exercise of love" declared to be the means God uses to develop likeness to Christ in us, His children. Holiness expresses itself purely in the love of God, therefore to walk in love, is to walk towards holiness. Holiness is the very presence of God, because He lives in holiness.

Wherever the presence of God is, "holiness is evident." To live in holiness, is to know God, because it is His very nature. Holiness is characterized by a progressive and consistence separation of a believer unto God. It is to live a consistence sanctified life, and to maintain a relationship with God. It is to imitate the life of Christ, which is the life of holiness.

The presence of God is a presence of holiness; you can't comfortably stay there, if you are not sanctified! Exod. 3:5

◆•••◆

Holiness is not an option! It is an absolute and a must, before partnership with God can happen! Lev. 11:45

◆•••◆

Holiness is a product of obedience; to attain it, is to walk in obedience! Deut. 28:11

◆•••◆

The holiness of God is incomparable! It takes a heart of gratitude to understand that! 1 Sam. 2:2

◆•••◆

If you want God to accept your offering and worship; then you must be ready to do it in an act of holiness! Ps. 93:5

◆ • ◆

It is holiness that will make your Christian life look bright! Without it, you will look so dull and dim! Ps. 110:3

◆ • ◆

Purity before God is an access to favour with people! Gen. 39:21-23

◆ • ◆

Separation unto God is the easiest way to holiness! Lev. 21:8

◆ • ◆

Purity of heart is what guarantees your unlimited access to God, and all His goodness; it is not your outward appearance. Matt. 5:8

◆••◆

Determine to live a lifestyle of righteousness, and holiness will emerge in your life! Rom. 6:19

◆••◆

Without Christ being in the centre of your life; "forget about holiness", it is not possible! 1 Cor. 1:30

◆••◆

Sexual immorality is the biggest enemy to a holy lifestyle! Fight against it with everything you have within you! 1 Thes. 4:3, 4

◆••◆

Holiness is part of the qualification to a saved life! Without it, salvation is incomplete! 1 Tim. 2:15

◆••◆

Have you come to a stage in your Christian walk, where people have rejected you? "Don't worry, take courage", God is moulding you to become more like Him in holiness! 1 Pet. 2:4, 5

◆•••••••••••••••••••••••••••••◆

You must first buy your ticket to deliverance, before you start your journey to holiness! Obad. 1:17

◆•••••••••••••••••••••••••••••◆

Holiness is a product of deliverance, deliverance is a product of obedience, obedience is a product of the truth, the truth is found in the word of God, the word of God is Jesus! John 1:1-3, 8:32

◆•••••••••••••••••••••••••••••◆

Holiness has no age trace! It is as old as God Himself! Rev. 4:8

◆•••••••••••••••••••••••••••••••••••••◆

Until you separate yourself from the worldly lifestyle; holiness for you will continue to be a struggle! 2 Cor. 6:14-17

◆•••••••••••••••••••••••••••••••••••••◆

Holiness has eternal reward! Do your best to be part of the reward! 2 Pet. 3:11-14

◆•••••••••••••••••••••••••••••••••••••◆

Your body is a dwelling place for God; don't do anything that will shut Him out! 1 Cor. 3:16, 17

◆•••••••••••••••••••••••••••••••••••••◆

Our faith is a holy faith, we don't have to apologise for it! Jude 20

◆•••••••••••••••••••••••••••••••••••••◆

When it comes to holiness, there is no negotiation of it to those who want to be a part of the family of God, it's a must! 1 Pet. 1:15, 16

◆ • ◆

Holiness is associated with discipline; if you don't want to be disciplined, forget about holiness! Heb. 12:10

◆ • ◆

You will do anything to stay pure and live a holy life; by the time you understand the great blessings and wonderful benefit that comes out of it! 2 Cor. 7:1

◆ • ◆

If you make the Holy Spirit your best companion; living a holy life will become a normal life to you! 2 Thes. 2:13

◆ • ◆

If you want to experience God, and His power in your life, then be ready to meet His condition; it is found in holiness. Heb. 12:14

◆••◆

For you to continue to be in touch with God; you need a consistence sanctified lifestyle! Eph. 4:22-24

◆••◆

Christ is coming soon for those who are waiting for Him in purity! Are you among them? 1 John 3:2, 3

8

Love is the Greatest

*L*ove is a four letter word that is so powerful and can change any tough situation, can change the lives of people, if it is well appropriated. "God is love" and if you know Him, you know love. There are different types of love that the world knows, but the one I am talking about here is the one that flows from God, and it is called the "Agape Love."

Agape! Is from the Greek word called "Agapao." It is a word in the New Testament used to describe the attitude of God toward the entire human race! (John 3:16) Agape as the love from God, also conveys "His will to His children", concerning their attitude towards one another, and towards all men. God's love is seen in the gift of His Son and this love had its perfect expression among men in the person of the Lord Jesus Christ.

The agape of God also manifested in the Old Testament where we see the dealings of God towards His people, and how He wants them to express His agape towards one another. The agape love, when given is impossible to be refused! This love is irresistible, it is irreplaceable, it is irrepressible, it is so incredible and on and on ..... This kind of love is very difficult for you to give to people, if you are a selfish person. This kind of love comes from God alone, and He is the only one who can help you to give it to people.

If you want people to see God in you, give them this love. This love is the love that does not keep account of the wrong things done by people. This love does not rejoice when bad things happen to other peoples. This love does not take offence when offended. This love does not insult when insulted, it is not proud and rude. This love is not suspicious, but it is clear and clean in expression. This love is called the love of God. (Read 1 Cor. 13:1-13)

Not returning "evil for evil, but good for evil" can only happen where God's kind of love is in operation! Lev. 19:18

◆• •◆

Until you love God with all the three dimensions that make up you; your walk with Him is questionable! Deut. 6:5

◆• •◆

You can't love God; until you fully understand that He is the reason why you are living! Ps. 18:1, 2

◆• •◆

It is only your love for God that will cause you to love His word! Ps. 119:97

◆• •◆

Your real identity will show up! By the time you love the people who don't deserve it! Matt. 5:44, 45

◆••••••••••••••••••••••••••••••••••••••◆

It is your whole love for a "whole God" that will take you to your second part of your love walk with Him; which is to love other people! Matt. 22:37-39

◆••••••••••••••••••••••••••••••••••••••◆

Determine to walk in love with the people of God; and you will be a true representative of Christ, here on earth! John 13:34, 35

◆••••••••••••••••••••••••••••••••••••••◆

To hate what is bad and love what is good, is a sign of true love! Rom. 12:9

◆••••••••••••••••••••••••••••••••••••••◆

Your life will become the abode of God; when you love Jesus Christ, His only begotten Son! John 14:23

◆••••••••••••••••••••••••••••••••••••••◆

If your lifestyle is always an offence to other peoples, it is a sign that you are not rooted in love! Rom. 13:10

◆•••••••••••••••••••••••••••••••••••••◆

It is a curse to say that you are a Christian, and not love the Lord Jesus Christ, whose name you are bearing! 1 Cor. 16:22

◆•••••••••••••••••••••••••••••••••••••◆

It is your love for God, that will cause you to put your faith in Him; and as a result, your salvation is certain! 1 Pet. 1:8, 9

◆•••••••••••••••••••••••••••••••••••••◆

You cannot love the world and God at the same time; if you do, your life will be full of confusion! 1 John 2:15

◆•••••••••••••••••••••••••••••••••••••◆

To say that you love God, without loving people around you, is a lie and a personal deception! For the love of God is for all! 1 John 4:7-10

◆......................................◆

Love will affect everything you do; if you understand the power that is in love. 1 Cor. 16:14

◆......................................◆

When God's type of love controls your lifestyle; your struggle with sin will be a thing of the past! 2 Cor. 5:14

◆......................................◆

When you try the love of God that flows through Christ; you will be amazed at what your discovery will be! Eph. 3:19

◆......................................◆

We are not accepted by God, through what we have done; but by our faith in Christ, that is found in love! Gal. 5:16

◆ • ◆

Giving up your life for the sake of others, will not be a difficult thing for you; if you operate in Christ-type of love. Eph. 5:2

◆ • ◆

If you let the love of Christ in you go out to other people; your boldness before God is guaranteed! 1 Thes. 3:12, 13

◆ • ◆

Until you have a genuine and God's type of love operating in your life; fear will continue to torment your life! 1 John 4:18

◆ • ◆

If you want to keep the whole of God's commandment; then walk in love, and you will be able to do that! Gal. 5:14

◆••••••••••••••••••••••••••••••••••••••◆

Love is the only driving force to forgiveness and the fountain that waters our Christian life; without it, we will be so dry and empty! Col. 3:12-14

◆••••••••••••••••••••••••••••••••••••••◆

To show undivided love for the Lord, and the things of God, is a serious business; make sure you understand it very well before you venture! John 21:15-19

◆••••••••••••••••••••••••••••••••••••••◆

To live a life of love towards other people is a hard work; but it has a great eternal reward! Heb. 6:10-12

◆••••••••••••••••••••••••••••••••••••••◆

It is only love that will help you to have a steady relationship with other Christians; without it, you will have a lot of frustration! 1 Pet. 4:8

◆••••••••••••••••••••••••••••••••••◆

Your continuous love toward other Christians will lead you into doing unusual things for them; which will bring unusual blessings in your life! Heb. 13:1, 2

◆••••••••••••••••••••••••••••••••••◆

When you understand how deep the love of God is for your life; then you will be able to face anything that comes your way! 2 Thes. 3:5

◆••••••••••••••••••••••••••••••••••◆

Being obedient to the word of God; is your first step toward your love walk with Him. 1 John 2:5

◆•••◆

Love is like a seed that grows; but you have to first sow it and then it will germinate and after grow to become a big useful tree! 2 Pet. 1:7, 8

◆•••◆

The biggest evidence of someone's changed life; is the manifestation of love in his or her life. 1 Pet. 1:22

◆•••◆

The love of God towards us is so much that our mind cannot fathom! It is better than the love of our earthly father! 1 John 3:1

◆•••◆

If you can't love people that you see! How can you love God that you did not see? It is not just possible! 1 John 4:20

NOTES

9

Jesus is the Way

Jesus! From the Hebrew word "Joshua", which means "Jehovah is saviour" or "Jehovah is salvation". Jesus! A name that was given to the Son of God in incarnation as His personal name. It was given to Him in obedience to the command of an angel to Joseph, the husband of His mother, Mary, shortly before He was born. Jesus who is also called Christ, is the anointed of God, and was made known openly as the "Messiah", after His resurrection from the dead.

It is a wonderful thing to know that Jesus Christ as the anointed one of God, has been from the very beginning of all things. Jesus was first revealed to the prophets of God before He was revealed to

His apostles and is revealed to us today as the saviour of the world. The prophets saw Him as the embodiment of all the characteristics of God. They saw Him as the one who was going to later usher in all the attributes of God, to the troubled world. They saw Him as the peace of God, the love of God, the mercy of God, the justice of God and above all the saviour of the world.

Life without Jesus Christ, is a life full of crises. If you are looking for peace, find Jesus first, then you will have peace, because He is the Prince of Peace. Jesus is the love of God in action, He is the love of God fulfilled, He is the epitome of the love of God. Without Jesus, it will be impossible for us to show people love because He is the one who gives us His Holy Spirit, which helps us to love other people.

Jesus is the only one who possesses the greatest and the most honourable title both in heaven and on earth! Isaiah 9:6, 7

◆•••••••••••••••••••••••••••••••••••◆

The primary mission that Jesus came here to do, is to save His people, and that includes me and you! Matt. 1:21

◆•••••••••••••••••••••••••••••••••••◆

Jesus! The man who walks on top of water without sinking! Matt. 14:25

◆•••••••••••••••••••••••••••••••••••◆

Jesus! The word of God spoken of from the very beginning as the seed of the word of God; is God Himself, and history revealed! John 1:1-3

◆•••••••••••••••••••••••••••••••••••◆

Jesus! God of heaven who came in the flesh like us, in order to identify with us! John 1:14

◆ • ◆

The glory of God was seen physically by many people when Jesus was here on earth, and can still be seen again in the life of those who receive Him as their lord and saviour! Isaiah 40:5

◆ • ◆

Jesus is our light and salvation! Without Him, we will be lost forever! Isaiah 49:6

◆ • ◆

Jesus! The only road that leads to God, you cannot get to God, until you travel through Him! John 14:6

◆ • ◆

To be fruitful in your Christian life is to stay put in Jesus! John 15:4

◆•••◆

The miraculous power in the name of Jesus, is better than ordinary alms or money. Acts 3:4-8

◆•••◆

What manner of man is this Jesus? He ate and drank with the man who was going to betray Him! Can you do that? Matt. 26:21-23

◆•••◆

What manner of man is this Jesus? He prayed for the people, who nailed and crucified Him; this is incredible! Luke 23:34

◆•••◆

Jesus! The man who touched the untouchable in his days and healed him, because of His love and compassion! Matt. 8:3

◆••◆

Jesus came here for a very simple but powerful mission; it is to defeat the enemy and to give us life in abundance! John 10:10

◆••◆

Jesus! The only man who has the power to change the atmosphere and His appearance at any time! Luke 9:28-32

◆••◆

Jesus! The only man who has a divine confirmation to his baptism and position, as the Son of God! Matt. 3:16, 17

◆••◆

To overcome the darkness of this evil world; is to follow Jesus who is the light of the world! John 8:12

◆•••••••••••••••••••••••••••••••••••◆

You cannot come in contact with Jesus and still be the same person! Acts 9:3-6

◆•••••••••••••••••••••••••••••••••••◆

Jesus is the only truth strong enough to set anyone free from all the errors in this life! John 8:32

◆•••••••••••••••••••••••••••••••••••◆

You can never have victory over sin and death without Jesus! Rom. 5:17

◆•••••••••••••••••••••••••••••••••••◆

You will cross barrier and boundaries, when you say what Jesus had said already! Mark 11:6

◆•••••••••••••••••••••••••••••••••••◆

Jesus is no more here physically; but spiritually He is with those who believe and put their trust in Him! Mark 16:17-20

◆••••••••••••••••••••••••••••••••••••••◆

It is only those who believe and make Jesus their personal lord and saviour that are qualified to be God's children! John 1:12

◆••••••••••••••••••••••••••••••••••••••◆

Not believing in Jesus, is the greatest sin anyone can commit; this kind of sin has eternal consequences! John 3:36

◆••••••••••••••••••••••••••••••••••••••◆

Only through the name of Jesus can anyone be saved! There is no other! Acts 4:12

◆••••••••••••••••••••••••••••••••••••••◆

Jesus! The man who secured our salvation with His own blood; nobody could have done that! Heb. 9:12

◆••◆

It takes only a ready and a humble heart to understand who "this Jesus really is." John 9:39

◆••◆

Do you want a friend that will be there for you anytime, anywhere, in good time and bad time? Then find Jesus! He is a friend that stays closer better than a brother. Prov. 18:24

◆••◆

To have the power of God in your life as a Christian is to imitate the life of Christ Jesus! Phil. 2:5-11

◆••◆

For you to keep going and standing as a Christian, don't ever lose the sight of Jesus; otherwise you will fall by the sight of all the things around you! Heb. 12:2

◆••◆

Jesus! The only man capable of taking away the sins of the whole world! John 3:29

◆••◆

Jesus! The only man who used five loaves of bread and two fish to feed five thousand men. Matt. 14:15-21

◆••◆

Death is nothing in the presence of Jesus, for He is the resurrection and the life! John 11:25

◆••◆

Jesus! The man who has never changed, will never change, and can never change! What do you say? Heb. 13:8

NOTES

10

Prayer is the Key

Prayer is a way we communicate with God, both in talking to Him and listening to Him. Prayer is a powerful tool of communication with God, and our divine access to Him and His access to us. It is our only spiritual telephone to heaven, the abode of God. Prayer is the only line of divine communication God has established between heaven and earth, between us and Him.

Nothing comes down from heaven to earth, except through the channel of prayer. It is the only divine vehicle capable of bringing down heavenly loads from heaven to earth. Just as there is a right and wrong way to communicate with people around us, and the right and the wrong way to communicate with your telephone to a friend, so there is also the right and wrong way to communicate with God.

If you pick up your telephone to call your friend, and on the process dialled the wrong number, there is not going to be any communication because you have just dialled the wrong number. If there is no communication, there would not be any reply or answer because communication has not taken place.

God has established a principle of communication with Him, if we want our communication with Him to be productive. The principle of God is in dialling the right number when trying to communicate with Him. Dialling the right number always starts by using the name of Jesus, when trying to communicate with God, and the rest follows.

God guarantees His blessing to anybody who prays according to His will. Ps. 122:6

◆••••••••••••••••••••••••••••••••••••••◆

It is only a fool that does not know the value of praying to God! Job 21:15

◆••••••••••••••••••••••••••••••••••••••◆

Right-standing with God, guarantees His answer to your prayers, keep it up! Prov. 15:29

◆••••••••••••••••••••••••••••••••••••••◆

Where there is a broken heart, God is there ready to help! Ps. 34:18

◆••••••••••••••••••••••••••••••••••••••◆

Unconfessed sin is dangerous! It closes God's ear from listening to you, when you call on Him! Ps. 66:18

◆••••••••••••••••••••••••••••••••••••••◆

Until you deal with the issue of sin in your life; you will never understand the true meaning of prayer! Isaiah 59:1-3

◆ • ◆

It takes a humble and repentant heart to know the greatness of God, during the time of prayer! Dan. 9:3-5

◆ • ◆

If you are not ready to forgive people their sins against you; forget about prayer, it doesn't make sense! Matt. 6:14, 15

◆ • ◆

There is a sure confidence given to us in the word of God concerning whatever we ask for, even in prayer! Gal. 4:7

◆ • ◆

God is not impressed by a long prayer; the only thing he wants is to be believed! Matt. 21:21, 22

◆••◆

If you are not a consistent and a stable person; you will always score zero, when it comes to the subject of prayer! Luke 18:1-8

◆••◆

When your desire is to show forth the glory of God through your prayers, He will definitely show up when you call Him! 1 Kings 18:36-39

◆••◆

Our prayers are powerful enough to put the angels to work on our behalf! Acts 12:5-7

◆••◆

If you make prayer your lifestyle; it will become a solution for troubles to you at any time! Dan. 6:10

◆••◆

If you are not ready to turn from your wicked ways when you pray, the "devil" will mock your prayers, God will not answer! 2 Chron. 7:14

◆••◆

Prayer is not sending God on an errand for you! It is getting you to do the will of God! Jas. 4:3

◆••◆

No matter how long and how many times you pray, the will of God is what is important at the end! Matt. 26:39-46

◆••◆

Invite the Holy Spirit, when you don't know what to say in your prayer; He is the only one who knows your mind and the mind of God! Rom. 8:26

◆••◆

Anytime you are faced with a fearful situation in your life; the best thing to do is to call upon God in prayer! Acts 27:29

◆••◆

Prayer is a spiritual weapon! Train yourself on how to use it at any time! 2 Cor. 4-6

◆••◆

Prayer is more effective when it is done out of a pure and a clean heart! 1 Tim. 2:8

◆••◆

When sin is exposed, prayer becomes more powerful to accomplish anything! Jas. 5:16

◆ • ◆

One of the quickest ways to receive things from God in prayer is through agreement with others! Matt 18:19

◆ • ◆

When your prayer is in accordance with the will of God; He will surely send you an aid to accomplish His will! Luke 22:41-43

◆ • ◆

Prayer of unity is powerful! The enemy cannot stand it! Acts 4:24

◆ • ◆

You can never accomplish anything by worrying! But with prayers, sky will never limit you! Phil. 4:6

◆• •◆

It is a heart of compassion that will cause you to pray for other people's need, even when you are in need yourself! 2 Cor. 13:7

◆• •◆

Our enemy operates in the secret, so we must operate in our secret dimension of prayer against Him. Eph. 6:18

◆• •◆

In whatever situation you find yourself in, good or bad, keep on praying! 1 Thes. 5:17, 18

◆• •◆

Prayer is a hard work! But it is so rewarding! Heb. 5:7

◆••••••••••••••••••••••••••••••••••••••◆

Prayer is a time when burdens change shoulders! <u>Righteous Rule</u>

◆••••••••••••••••••••••••••••••••••••••◆

God is powerful enough to do anything; but He is waiting for us to call upon Him in prayer! Acts 12:5-8

◆••••••••••••••••••••••••••••••••••••••◆

No matter how strong or powerful you are spiritually; you will need the prayer of other saints of God sometimes to keep you standing! Heb. 13:18

◆••••••••••••••••••••••••••••••••••••••◆

When your prayer is mixed with praises unto God; you have entered a dimension

of power, and anything can happen!
Acts 16:25, 26

◆••◆

Murmuring and complaining against
leaders is a business that yields no profit,
pray for them instead! 1 Tim. 2:1-5

◆••◆

Jesus started and is still continuing with
prayers! Why can't we do the same?
Heb. 7:25

NOTES

11

Speak the Word of God!

There is an immense power that is available to us, when we speak the word of God. Having an understanding that there is an immense power in the word of God, when we speak it in our lives or any situation we are faced with, will help us to see things in a different perspective.

There is power in a spoken word of God; it has such a power to turn things around for our good. We are responsible for whatever happens in our lives as a result of the words we speak. Are we speaking the words of God, which are words full of faith, or are we speaking the words of the "enemy the devil", which are words full of fear and torment? Word! From the Greek word "logos" which denotes the expression of thought and not the mere name of an object. It is also the embodiment of a conception or idea.

The word "logos" can become a "rhema" when attributed to God. The significance of this is that the word "logos" moves from the place of ordinary or common, to a place of "rhema", which makes it extraordinary and powerful to be able to accomplish something.

As believers in Christ Jesus, we are admonished to speak the "logos rhema" of God in our lives. We are supposed to speak the "logos rhema" of God concerning any situation we are faced with, knowing that the spoken word of God carries power with it. This will encourage us to speak those words, for God created this world with a spoken word.

God is the eternal creator, who spoke the first ever word, when He spoke this world into existence, where there was nothing! Gen. 1:1-3

◆••◆

It is better to keep your mouth shut, if you are not sure about what to say! Because whatever you say whether good or bad will come to pass! Prov. 18:21

◆••◆

Your obedience to the word of God will cause you to be distinguished from other people! Deut. 4:6, 7

◆••◆

Teach the word of God to your children; it has the power to shape their lives as they grow up! 2 Tim. 3:15

◆••◆

The word of God is perfect; you can depend upon it to sustain your life! Ps. 19:7

◆•••◆

There are no contradictions in the word of God; you can count on it at any time! Ps. 119:160

◆•••◆

Speak the word of God, and sinners will be convicted of their sins and ask for help! Acts 2:37

◆•••◆

Your salvation is questionable! If you are ashamed of speaking the word of God to other people! Rom. 1:16

◆•••◆

*Your duty is to speak the word of God;
His duty is to confirm the word in the
heart of the people! 1 Thes. 2:13*

◆••◆

*If it takes you crying out, for you to be
fed with the word of God; please do it, for
your own benefit! 1 Pet. 2:2*

◆••◆

*If you are waiting for the perfect time,
before you speak the word of God; it may
never come, now is the time! 2 Tim. 4:2*

◆••◆

*Once the word of God is spoken over
anything, that thing is bound to respond
to the word of God, whatever it is! Isaiah
55:11*

◆••◆

The word of God is foolishness to those who are on their way to destruction; but to those who have believed in it, it is the power of God, enough to save them! 1 Cor. 1:18

◆•••••••••••••••••••••••••••••••••••••◆

Before anything existed, the word of God has always been, and will ever be, because that word is God Himself, who outlived everything! 1 John 1:1

◆•••••••••••••••••••••••••••••••••••••◆

The word of God is the only thing that has the power to travel to an unknown and unlimited distance! Heb. 4:12

◆•••••••••••••••••••••••••••••••••••••◆

When you cultivate a habit of studying the word of God and make it your best companion, you have set yourself on the path to success! Josh. 1:8

◆ • ◆

The amount of the word of God you have stored in your heart will determine how far you will have victory over sin! Ps. 119:11

◆ • ◆

The word of God has enough power to give you direction in the darkest time of your life and to show you which way to turn next! Ps. 119:105

◆ • ◆

When the "devil" speaks his deceitful words to you, "don't be silent", speak back the word of God to him and he will be on the run! Luke 4:12, 13

◆ • ◆

The spoken word of God is older and stronger than death itself. John 2:22

◆••••••••••••••••••••••••••••••••••••••◆

The word of God is the only thing that is tastier and sweeter than any other thing in life. Ps. 119:103

◆••••••••••••••••••••••••••••••••••••••◆

When you find the word of God; you have found the greatest treasure in this life. Ps. 119:162

◆••••••••••••••••••••••••••••••••••••••◆

Though everything we see may fail or disappoint us; the word of God will never fail. Isaiah 40:8

◆••••••••••••••••••••••••••••••••••••••◆

As soon as you understand the power that is contained in a spoken word of God; the easier it is for you to receive something from Him! Luke 7:7

◆••••••••••••••••••••••••••••••••••••••◆

The word of God embedded in our heart, is a spiritual weapon we have, to fight the enemy! Are you equipped with it? Eph. 6:17

NOTES

12

Obedience and Blessings

Obedience is the very act of obeying or willingness to obey; it is to obey what you are told to do, and to carry out an instruction. The most noble and blessed thing anyone can do in this life, is to be obedient to what he or she knows is true and good. That which is good always starts with God, who is a giver of all good things.

That which is blessed, originated only from God, because He is a God of blessings. Obedience in various aspects of life always starts with obeying God, who has established its very condition and boundaries.

Obedience is of the conduct and may be observed, "and blessing is the only thing hidden in obedience." When a man obeys God, he gives the only possible evidence that in his heart he believes God. While a good and blessed life is a result of obedience; troubles and pain and all sorts of bad things most of the time are direct consequences of disobedience.

Blessings come as a result of obedience, obedience is the result of diligence, diligence is the result of hearkening, and hearkening unto the voice of God. Deut. 28:1-6

◆••••••••••••••••••••••••••••••••••••••◆

True obedience to God has a rule; it is to respond without delay! Gen. 22:2, 3

◆••••••••••••••••••••••••••••••••••••••◆

Pharaoh of Egypt was a good example of delayed obedience, for he paid dearly for it! Exod. 12:28-31

◆••••••••••••••••••••••••••••••••••••••◆

Obedience to God and His word is the only key to distinction! Deut. 4:6

◆••••••••••••••••••••••••••••••••••••••◆

It is only obedience to the word of God that guarantees the succession of His blessings in your life and your children after you! 1 Kings 2:2-4

◆•••••••••••••••••••••••••••••••••••••••◆

Obedience carries life and blessings; but disobedience is an agent of death and destructions! Job 36:11, 12

◆•••••••••••••••••••••••••••••••••••••••◆

You can never substitute obedience with any other thing, it doesn't work! 1 Sam. 15:22

◆•••••••••••••••••••••••••••••••••••••••◆

Obedience to God is the only source of true happiness in this life! Ps. 119:56

◆•••••••••••••••••••••••••••••••••••••••◆

Listening to the word of God, without obeying it does not make any sense, it's only an illusion! Jas. 1:22, 23

◆•••••••••••••••••••••••••••••••••••••••◆

It will be difficult for you to stay pure without being obedient to the word of God! Ps. 119:9

◆•••◆

God is ever ready to help those who obey Him; but those who disobey Him are in constant danger of destruction! Isaiah 1:19, 20

◆•••◆

There is nothing good about disobedience, it only makes life miserable! Isaiah 42:24

◆•••◆

Obedience to God is the only thing that leads to true promotion and honour in life, try it! Deut. 28:1

◆•••◆

To trust and obey, is the only way to be happy in Christ, and the only way to bring glory to Him! Rom. 1:5

◆••••••••••••••••••••••••••••••••••••◆

Whatever you obey will determine what you are going to have, "life or death"- the choice is yours! Rom. 6:16

◆••••••••••••••••••••••••••••••••••••◆

You cannot deal solidly with the issue of disobedience, until you yourself have fully obeyed! 2 Cor. 10:6

◆••••••••••••••••••••••••••••••••••••◆

Obedience to our parents is a confirmation of our obedience to God and this is the way to a blessed life! Eph. 6:1

◆••••••••••••••••••••••••••••••••••••◆

Obedience to God is the only thing that leads to a true greatness in life! Phil. 2:8-10

◆・・◆

Until you fully obey God; you will never know what a true rest in Him is all about! Heb. 3:18

◆・・◆

To discover the great love of God, is to love and obey His word! Exod. 20:6

◆・・◆

The secret of the best position to everything in life is found in obedience to the word of God, discover it! Deut. 28:13

◆・・◆

Refusing to obey what you know is the truth, does not do you any good at all; it only brings continuous anger of God upon your life. Rom. 2:8

◆•••••••••••••••••••••••••••••••••••••••◆

God is committed to doing anything whenever He sees obedience, even if it is from only one person! Are you the one? Rom. 5:19

◆•••••••••••••••••••••••••••••••••••••••◆

If you still have struggle when it comes to giving; it is a sign that you are not totally obedient to the word of God! 2 Cor. 9:13

◆•••••••••••••••••••••••••••••••••••••••◆

Don't ever let anything stand between you and your obedience to God, whatever it is! Acts 5:29

◆•••••••••••••••••••••••••••••••••••••••◆

Disobedience will only cause you injuries and great loss; try your very best to avoid it. Acts 27:21

◆•••◆

When your obedience to God is sincere and unreserved, He will surely bless you for that! Phil. 2:12

◆•••◆

Disobedience is contagious, don't let it infect you; but overcome it with obedience. 2 Thes. 3:14, 15

◆•••◆

God can never abandon those who obey Him! Are you one of them? Ps. 119:8

◆•••◆

To remain in the love of Christ is to continue obeying Him! John 15:10

◆•••◆

Do you want your life to go very smoothly? Then be ready to obey the spiritual leaders that God has put in your path! Heb. 13:17

◆•••◆

Disobedience to the law of the Lord is as the same as disobedience to God, there is no difference! Rom. 13:1, 2

◆•••◆

One of the best ways to learn about obedience, is through suffering, don't run away from it! Heb. 5:8

◆•••◆

By the time you understand who you really are in God, then it will not be difficult for you to obey Him! 1 Pet. 1:14

◆•••◆

Here comes the conclusion of the whole matter! It is to fear God and obey His word, for this is the only way to have a blessed and fulfilled life, there is no other way! Eccl. 12:13

Shalom!!!

If this book has been a blessing to you, please share your testimony with the author.

Contact:
Phone: +353 87 282 0197, +353 87 953 3613

Emails: Ezekiel@faithrestoration.info,
        hisjustice@ymail.com

Write to:
23 Melrose Avenue,
Fairview,
Dublin 3.
Ireland.

About the Author

E. J. Ezekiel, a vibrant brother in the Lord. He has a warmth and dynamic heart for the service of the Lord Jesus Christ. He holds an associate degree in theology and a diploma in the school of ministry. He is currently in Victory Christian Fellowship, one of the biggest evangelical churches in the Republic of Ireland, where he is involved in a loving help to the ministry.

NOTES

NOTES

NOTES

NOTES